A Murmuration of Starlings

THE COLLECTIVE NOUNS OF ANIMALS AND BIRDS

This book is dedicated
with love to my wife Cathy
and son Michael

A Murmuration of Starlings

THE COLLECTIVE NOUNS OF ANIMALS AND BIRDS

Written and illustrated by
Steve Palin

MERLIN UNWIN BOOKS

First published by Merlin Unwin Books, 2013

Text and illustrations © Steve Palin 2013

Merlin Unwin Books Limited
Palmers' House, 7 Corve Street,
Ludlow, Shropshire, SY8 1DB
www.merlinunwin.co.uk

A CIP record of this book is available from the British Library.

Printed and bound by 1010 Printing International Ltd

ISBN 9781906122546

Introduction

Most people are familiar with the term a flock of birds, some with a skein of geese or even a covey of partridge, but how many of us would know the company term for a group of woodpeckers or woodcock?

Collective nouns were first recorded with authority in *The Book of St Albans* of 1486, purportedly by the Prioress Dame Juliana Berners, in which the lists were entitled 'The Compaynys of Beestys and Fowlys'. Her book relied for much of its information on another work: *Le Art de Venerie* (sic) by William Twici, published circa 1328. Twici was Edward II's huntsman and this is the oldest known hunting book in England. It was reprinted in 1843 and in the intervening period there were many other books on the subject. My compilation today uses many of these historic entries, some important modern additions and my illustrations.

A collective noun is a word which describes a group or collection of things, variously called a company term, a group term or a noun of assembly. Not all apply to living creatures (for example a clutch of eggs), but those that do are some of the most interesting, both in terms of the word itself and also of its origins.

The origins of such collective nouns generally fall into four categories:
- true company terms
- terms which represent the young or progeny
- terms which represent bird or animal characteristics
- terms which represent bird or animal noises or cries

Some, however, are entirely fanciful and yet others are the result of mis-copying by scribes before the days of the printing press. Many of these nouns which apply to living creatures were first recorded in the manuscripts of the Middle Ages, when social etiquette, particularly on the occasion of a hunt, demanded their correct usage. It is those creatures associated with the hunt (rather than those particularly inclined to be gregarious) which have the richest collectives nouns applied to them and which the hunting fraternity has kept alive even today.

There is little doubt that in those early days, scribes and printers were guilty of some mis-copying. Together with the natural evolution of language, this gave rise to variations of terms which, although phonetically similar, may be semantically quite different; for example, the group term for herons and bitterns is recorded as a siege or a sedge.

Lists of collective nouns today appear in many different volumes: schoolchildren's grammar books, crossword companions, anthologies and so on. In my experience no two such lists are alike; words which are contained in one may be missed out from another. The list which appears at the back of this book is a compilation of every group term for birds and animals known to me, provided they have withstood the test of time.

This little book is not intended to be an academic work. Books such as C.E. Hare's *The Language of Sport* (1939) and James Lipton's *An Exaltation of Larks* or *The Venereal Game* (1970) have given the academic perspective on this subject. Rather, this work is intended to be fun.

Steve Palin, September 2013

A Parliament of Owls

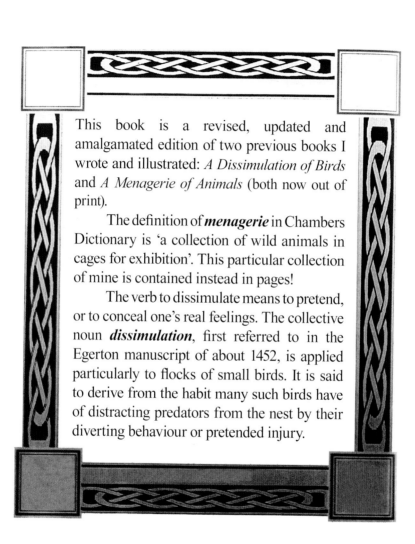

This book is a revised, updated and amalgamated edition of two previous books I wrote and illustrated: *A Dissimulation of Birds* and *A Menagerie of Animals* (both now out of print).

The definition of **menagerie** in Chambers Dictionary is 'a collection of wild animals in cages for exhibition'. This particular collection of mine is contained instead in pages!

The verb to dissimulate means to pretend, or to conceal one's real feelings. The collective noun **dissimulation**, first referred to in the Egerton manuscript of about 1452, is applied particularly to flocks of small birds. It is said to derive from the habit many such birds have of distracting predators from the nest by their diverting behaviour or pretended injury.

Army of frogs and caterpillars

In his Glossary of 1828 Craven quotes *Bishop Hall's Contemplations*: 'he that hath brought **armies** of frogs and caterpillars to Egypt can as well bring whole drifts of birds and beasts to the desart' (sic). This seems to be the first written reference to this collective noun and it has subsequently stuck, appearing in many later lists up to the present day.

Although caterpillars are often found together in large numbers, this is largely owing to them having hatched from the egg together and having shared the same food plants, rather than any particular tendency towards gregarious company. The collective noun is more relevant, perhaps, to their purposeful 'marching' gait and the relentless laying waste of the vegetation on which they feed.

The application of the word to frogs is less convincing. Frogs can be gregarious and often group together in very large numbers, especially when mating, but the term army seems rather ill-matched. One theory is that it relates back to the plague of frogs in the bible which threatened a dynasty in the same way as might an army. An alternative collective noun for frogs is *colony*.

The common frog illustrated is the only species native to Britain. The caterpillars in the illustration are those of the puss-moth. When alarmed these beautiful creatures retract the head into their bodies and simultaneously display two large eye spots, wave a pair of red tentacles aggressively and shoot a jet of irritating fluid from a gland in their thorax. Just the sort of tactics you need from a member of the army!

ale of turtles

Turtles might not immediately strike one as being British animals, and certainly they do not breed anywhere in Britain. A number of species, however, are seen around the British coast. These include the illustrated Green turtle.

Although female marine turtles spend most of their lives in the sea, they must return to land to lay their eggs. They do this by digging holes on favoured, selected beaches and depositing up to 100 soft-shelled eggs deep in the sand and then covering them over. Even if all the eggs were to hatch, the baby turtles must then run the gauntlet of predators before reaching the relative sanctuary of the sea (where only their increased mobility and greater number of hiding places protect them from a further battery of predators). However, because the beaches to which the turtles return are readily identifiable, egg collecting for human consumption is rife. This, coupled with the demands of tourism, has consigned many species to the endangered list. *Bales* of turtles are certainly not of the number they once were.

The origin of the collective noun is something of a mystery, but there has been some detective work! The collective noun for doves is *dule* (this comes from the French *deuil* meaning mourning and relates to the mournful sound of the birds coo-ing). It is thought that early scribes not only mistook *turtle*-dove for the turtle itself, but they also corrupted *dule* to *bale*. There is currently no better explanation!

# ed of snakes

The references for the collective nouns of snakes are some of the scarcest. The author has found *bed* listed only in C.E. Hare's *The Language of Sport*, published in 1939. The other term, *den*, seems only to appear in the AA *Book of the British Countryside* list.

The words may serve to help reinforce many people's apparently innate but unjustified view of snakes - that of a cold, clammy serpent, poisonous and always ready to inflict harm on humans. But in fact, snakes are warm-blooded and dry. They shun human presence and are often shy and retiring. Most snakes of the world are non-poisonous. Three species are native to Britain, only one being poisonous; the adder or viper. The other two are the now rare smooth snake and the illustrated grass snake.

Adders are rich in folk-lore, particularly as a creature of ill-omen (a reference to a different type of serpent in the Garden of Eden). To come across one and let it live was supposedly to invite bad luck. Consequently, snakes of whatever species have historically been killed on sight. An ash stick was supposed to kill an adder instantly, whilst their cast skins reputedly had medicinal qualities: to wear one inside a hat prevented headaches and tied around one's leg it was protection against rheumatism. In the bible, Luke quotes John saying to the multitude: 'You brood of vipers!' The term is still in use today. A separate collective noun for the viper is nest.

The term *bed* has also been recorded as the collective noun for various shellfish, including clams, cockles, mussels and oysters. The latter has the term *hive* as an alternative.

*B*evy of quail

The collective noun for quails is long established. It was first recorded in the Egerton manuscript of the mid-fifteenth century and then in *The Book of St Albans* of 1486. *Bevy* is a true company term and has also been applied to larks, although C.E. Hare in *The Language of Sport* considers this may have been an error on the part of an early scribe. (*Bevy* is also recorded as a company term for roe deer and 'ladies' or 'beauties'!)

The quail is not only our smallest game bird, but also the only one which migrates. It spends the months from May to September breeding and raising its young here, before wintering in Africa. Many are shot and trapped during their journey over the Mediterranean and North African countries, and this is no doubt a factor in the quail's falling numbers. Although the British population can fluctuate from year to year, quail remain scarce and confine themselves mainly to the southern counties.

Quail are the antithesis to the stereotype of the model child, being more often heard than seen. They are shy, secretive birds, difficult to flush and seldom seen on the ground. They do, however, have a characteristic three-syllabled call, sometimes translated as 'wet-my-lips', which is persistently repeated at dawn and dusk. 'Wet-my-lips' is a local name for the quail in Norfolk.

Even in an area where quail are known to be, an opportunity to make use of the collective noun is rare; it is only on migration that the birds form small flocks. At other times they are usually solitary.

ast of hawks

The term ***cast*** is pure sporting terminology; it is used in relation only to birds ***cast*** from the fist in falconry or hawking. Moreover, the term relates only to a ***pair*** of birds being cast. If there were three, the group would be referred to as a ***leash***.

The word ***leash*** is also the specific collective noun for the 'ladies' falcon', or merlin. Goshawks too have their own specific term. The goshawk was the yeoman's bird, and was 'let fly' rather than cast. Its collective noun is consequently a ***flight*** of goshawks.

An alternative term for ***cast*** is ***couple***. This term may also be used for other birds of prey. ***Cast***, ***flight*** and ***leash*** (meaning three) appeared in *The Book of St Albans* in 1486. The use of ***leash*** as a term for merlin first appeared in another fifteenth-century manuscript written by Harley.

The birds illustrated are sparrowhawks; the larger brown female is in flight on the left and the smaller grey/blue male on the right. At one time only certain species of birds could be flown by particular social classes or groups, hence the title of the 1960s novel *A Kestrel for a Knave*.

Except for ***convocation***, a collective noun which is applied to eagles (of a somewhat questionable source), there seems to be no other collective noun for birds of prey apart from those above, which are falconry-related. This is despite the fact that many raptors are gregarious, often forming quite large groups.

ete of badgers

One of the best-loved of Britain's native wild animals, 'Brock' the badger still suffers from some persecution from badger-diggers. This, plus the claim that badgers carry bovine tuberculosis, together with an estimated death toll on Britain's roads of 50,000 animals per year prevents the badger from achieving the ubiquity that some may claim it deserves.

As well as the name 'bawsen', the badger was at one time called a 'gray' or 'grey' referring to its hair colour. Thus in many lists the company term is referred to as 'a *cete* of greys'. The origin of the term *cete* is unclear. It is possible that it is the old Chaucerian word for city, and this is accepted as a more likely justification for the collective noun than the other theory that it derives from the Latin word coetus meaning a meeting or assembly. *Cete* appeared first in the *Book of St Albans* in 1486, although a *syght* of badgers had appeared in the earlier Egerton manuscript probably in error.

It is fairly widely known that the badgers' home is called a set or sett, but this should not be confused with the collective noun. Chambers Dictionary distinctly defines *cete* as the collective noun for badgers and *set* as a badger's burrow. One list also records an alternative collective noun for badgers as a *colony*.

Badgers are part of the family of animals known as mustelids. This family includes otters, martens, stoats and weasels. The badger has left indelible marks on the British countryside in place names such as Brockham, Brockenhurst, Brockholes and many more.

harm of finches

The term *charm* is a particularly interesting one. Appearing first in the Egerton manuscript of the mid-fifteenth century as *chyrme*, and subsequently in *The Book of St Albans* as *cherme*, it is a variant of the Old English world *cirm*. It has many modern variations: the current dictionary definition of chirm, for example, is to chirp or chirrup like birds. Another definition is a group of goldfinches: certainly the term *charm* is commonly believed to refer to the *noise* produced by finches.

Whilst many collective nouns have fallen into almost total disuse, reference is still occasionally made to a *charm* of finches. Whilst one school of thought applies it exclusively to the illustrated goldfinch, another allows for its use for finches in general. (A *trimming* and a *trembling* are other collective nouns for goldfinches.)

Certainly it is appropriate to have a collective noun for finches. Finches generally, as well as goldfinches specifically, are highly gregarious. They often group together in large flocks, particularly outside the breeding season. The greater the food source, the larger the flock. They are often very vocal when in such groups, thus explaining the collective noun. Although many finches will form flocks of mixed finch species, the goldfinch usually associates only with others of its kind.

Finches are primarily seed-eating birds and the goldfinch is no exception, preferring the seeds of herbs and flowering plants to those of grasses. The goldfinch also prefers to eat half-ripe or *milky* seed to dried seed. It is common across most of the British Isles, but scarcer in the far north.

hime of wrens

Small in stature but big in heart, the wren must rank as one of Britain's favourite and most abundant birds. Its song in spring pours forth with such vigour that it can drown out those of much larger species. Our national bird, appearing on the old farthing coin, the wren is steeped in ritual and folklore. Not all of it is supportive of the wren; the once-traditional Yuletide Wren Hunt, for example, would seem to contradict its proclaimed place in our hearts.

Chime is only one of two collective nouns applied to the wren. The term *herd* is almost certainly the older (appearing in *The Book of St Albans* in 1486) and indeed the more common reference. One explanation for this latter term is that the wren was afforded the same noun of assembly as that used for the hart or royal stag, being considered a 'royal' bird itself: in the Greek story of the wren and the eagle, the wren cunningly outwits the eagle in a flying competition to earn the royal title of King of Birds. *Herd* is also the collective noun for curlew (see Herd of Curlew).

The term *chime*, relayed to the author but not referred to in any authoritative text, is perhaps a reference to the similarity between the bell-ringer's tones and the cascading notes or cadences of the wren.

The wren is at times gregarious: large numbers of wrens have been recorded together on migrational flights (migration activity takes place mainly at the northern extent of its range). The most interesting aspect of wrens grouping together, however, is during periods of cold weather, when numbers may huddle and roost together for warmth.

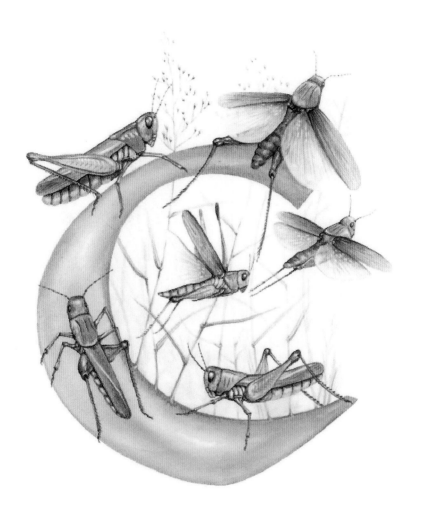

loud of grasshoppers

The term *cloud* applies to a number of insect species including the grasshopper. Those listed include flies, gnats and locusts. One of the dictionary definitions of the word *cloud* is 'a great number of things' and certainly it seems apt for those insects listed above, especially when some appear in ethereal masses dancing in the air. The grasshopper is, in fact, the least likely to be seen in the air. It usually only flies when disturbed, but nevertheless can arise from the grassy places where it predominantly lives in fair numbers, or *clouds*. C.E. Hare in his *The Language of Sport* also refers to a Dutch source who quotes a *swarm* of grasshoppers.

The grasshoppers in the illustration are Common Green Grasshoppers, which as their name implies are common across the British Isles. There are eleven British species of grasshopper, ten of which are able to fly. The flightless species is the Meadow Grasshopper and this is probably also the most common.

The 'singing' of grasshoppers is a common feature of summer days in the countryside. It is produced not by any vocal chords but by the grasshoppers' legs, which have small projections on their inner side. These are rubbed up and down against each other, producing a chirping or scraping sound. The action is called stridulating.

escent of woodpeckers

There are three species of resident British woodpecker: the great spotted, lesser spotted and the green. Of the three, the largest and most colourful is the illustrated green woodpecker. It is likely that the habits of this *particular* woodpecker gave rise to the company term, as it *descends* to the ground more frequently than the other two species. It does so to feed on its favourite food of ants, although sometimes it also feeds in trees. (Green woodpeckers have also been recorded *anting*, whereby the bird places ants amongst its feathers for the purpose of cleaning the plumage.)

The term ***descent*** may also arise from the ability of the green woodpecker to *descend* a tree, moving backwards down the trunk with its head uppermost. The third possible derivative of the term is the bird's occasional habit of moving from tree to tree, swooping downwards from the top of one to the base of another in the manner of a treecreeper.

Descent therefore is one of a number of collective nouns which relate to the habits or characteristics of a particular bird. The term was first recorded as ***discecion*** in a book called *The Hors, Shepe, & the Ghoos* printed in 1476 by Caxton.

One is unlikely to see a company of woodpeckers, however, as they are usually solitary birds. The exception to this general rule is perhaps during the breeding season when family groups may be seen in or around the nest site.

 # ray of squirrels

The word ***drey*** is fairly widely known as a term for the squirrel's nest. It has an alternative spelling of ***dray***, but this word is also the more usual, and certainly the earlier, spelling of the collective noun for the *young* of squirrels. Confusingly, however, this term is also sometimes spelt ***drey***.

The squirrel derives its name from its bushy tail which was once thought to serve as an umbrella; the Greek 'skia' meaning shade and 'oura' meaning tail.

Two members of the squirrel family are represented in Britain, the red and the grey. Only the red is indigenous. The grey is native to North America and its first recorded release was near Macclesfield in Cheshire in 1876. Further introductions followed and their subsequent range increased dramatically.

It has now displaced the red squirrel across most of England and Wales. It was thought until quite recently that the greys' aggression towards the red was largely responsible for the demise of the latter. The latest opinion, however, is that the grey has a much more robust constitution than the red. Its digestive system allows it to avail itself of a more diverse range of food. The red is also more prone to certain types of virus. These two factors combined mean that following natural downward population fluctuations, the grey is better able to capitalise within a particular habitat location, and over a period of time will become the dominant animal, ultimately excluding the red completely.

# arth of foxes

There are three collective nouns for foxes: *earth*, *skulk* and *leash*. The latter is a term applied to a group of just three foxes and is one of those collective nouns used for a wide range of animals and birds which are associated with the hunt in one form or another. The Egerton manuscript first listed the term *earth* as *nerthe* in 1452. The term is, of course, the name also applied to the fox's hole. The most commonly listed collective noun for foxes, *skulk*, was first recorded in *The Book of St Albans* in 1486 as *sculke*. The fox is not a gregarious animal and this term clearly relates to Reynard's stealthy prowling in search of its prey, traditionally around hen roosts!

In recent times the fox has extended its habitat to encompass towns and cities. The 'urban fox' is now a recognised descendant of its country cousin, living as an opportunist both in terms of its daytime resting places as well as its feeding habits, which often include scavenging in dustbins.

The fact that so many folk-tales include references to the cunning fox is evidence of our intrinsic liking for this cavalier animal.

A very popular country belief concerning foxes at one time was one which stated that to rid itself of fleas, the fox swam with a piece of lamb's wool in its mouth. To avoid drowning, the fleas would climb off the foxes body onto the wool, whereupon the fox would discard the wool together with the offending fleas. Scores of witnesses were reported to have verified this remarkable tale!

xaltation of larks

This evocative collective noun, dating from the fifteenth century, was used by James Lipton for the title of his 1968 book, *An Exaltation of Larks or The Venereal Game*. C.E. Hare, however, in his authoritative work, *The Language of Sport*, points out that the term is a fanciful, if long-standing name for larks in flight. Rather than being a true company term, it refers only to larks which soar into the sky and sing. The correct term for a number of larks is ***flight***, a term derived from the lark's characteristic behaviour when disturbed. Larks often socialise in large numbers.

There are many types of lark throughout the world. Only two have regularly nested in Britain: the skylark and the now rare woodlark. The illustrated shore lark (sometimes known in Lancashire as a *snowflake*) is a regular winter visitor to British coastlines but has only bred here sporadically. The ringed plover was once popularly termed the 'sand lark'. The corn bunting likewise was known as the 'scribbling lark', so named because of the pattern of 'scribbled' lines on its eggs. Neither of these birds, of course, is a true lark.

The larks most likely to be seen taking to the air to sing are skylarks. Our commonest lark, they are today experiencing a serious decline in numbers. Primarily responsible are the changing farming practices which affect the habitat in which they breed. At one time they were so common that they were killed in large numbers to eat, as well as being caged as songbirds. (They would often be blinded in the mistaken belief that their song would thus be improved.) It would indeed be a tragedy if the exultant song of this bird, once a ubiquitous feature of any spring walk in the countryside and the inspiration for countless poems, was lost to future generations.

all of woodcock

Woodcock are technically wading birds adapted to nesting and spending much of their time on the woodland and forest floor. The woodcock has long been a favourite sporting quarry, usually flushed by dog or beater as its camouflage inclines it to sit tight unless in immediate danger.

The term *fall* could refer both to its end of flight 'collapse' as it quickly drops to the ground and lands, or its reported habit of being sighted in numbers in the morning at places empty of woodcock the previous evening. (Woodcock are *crepuscular*, or active by dawn and dusk, so this phenomenon is quite feasible.) In this respect, reports that there had been a *fall of woodcock* would be in the same sense that there might have been a *fall of snow.*

Woodcock would not ordinarily be seen in groups, being typically solitary birds. There are times when more than one might be seen, however; for example, during a shoot where ground is being beaten, numbers of birds can often be seen in the air together. Whilst some woodcock are with us all year round, a degree of migratory movement does take place. Although they usually travel singly, they may occasionally be seen in pairs and very rarely in groups. In a good-sized wood, one can sometimes see and hear more than one woodcock performing their display flight, known as roding. They are, however, performing individually and not in a group.

Woodcock are so well camouflaged that it is sometimes difficult to see *one*, let alone many; for the birdwatcher, therefore, the collective noun for woodcock may only infrequently be required!

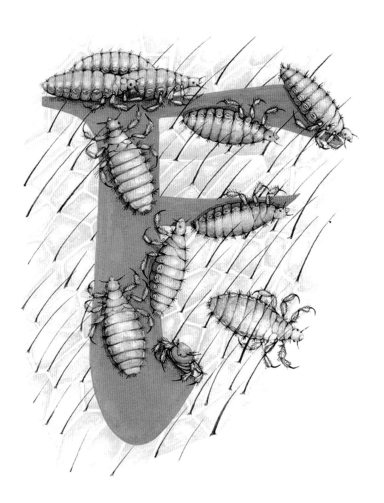

lock of lice

The Hors, Shepe, & the Ghoos is one of the earliest known books in England. It was printed by Caxton in 1476. The term *flock* as a collective noun for lice appeared in this volume, making it one of the earliest recorded nouns of assembly.

Flock is a term applied to a wide range of birds and animals including specifically camels, goats, sheep, lions (surprisingly) as well as beasts and birds generally. It is described by Hare as a 'true' company term (as opposed to a term which represents aspects of the creature itself). *Flock* also has relevance, of course, to humankind, and is applied to crowds of people generally and more particularly to congregations of church members.

The true louse is a wingless parasitic insect. It is quite unrelated to the booklouse, the woodlouse, the freshwater louse and their relative, the sea-slater, none of which are parasitic. Rarely more than 3 or 4 millimetres long, the two main types of louse are the biting lice and the sucking lice. Biting lice are found mainly (but not exclusively) on birds, whilst sucking lice prey on mammals.

Human beings are not excluded from the list of sucking lice host species, and the head louse (illustrated) is still commonly found in children's hair. Stories of the school 'nit nurse' still abound! The other species found on humans is the crab-louse, preferring body (and particularly pubic) hair in which to make its home, from which it will bore into the skin with its mouth parts to suck the blood from its host.

aggle of geese

The collective nouns for geese are similar to those for ducks in that both ducks and geese are collectively termed wildfowl. Thus the company terms *trip*, *sord*, *sute* and *plump* are common to both ducks and geese. *Gaggle* is a term specific to geese. Some authorities hold that it relates to geese only on land; others that it is those geese that are on land or water but not in the air. A number of geese in the air may be referred to as a *skein*, a *team* or a *wedge*. Mention has also been made of a *lag* of geese.

The term *gaggle* was first referred to as *gagelynge* in the Egerton manuscript of 1452. It has been claimed that it was one of those artificial and fanciful inventions of the fifteenth century, although it does refer to the noise made by geese. Its contemporary dictionary definition includes reference to a *knot* (see *knot* of waterfowl) of garrulous people, which can be likened to a flock of cackling geese. Whether fanciful or genuine, *gaggle* has stayed with us as a recognised term for geese when many other collectives have been lost through time.

The geese in the illustration are barnacle geese. These birds have a fascinating folklore. People at one time believed that they did indeed grow from barnacles. Medieval literature contains accounts of people claiming to be eyewitnesses to the hatching of the young geese from barnacle shells!

Barnacle geese are small grazing geese which breed in the Arctic and overwinter in Britain, mainly in Scotland and Ireland.

am of porpoises

Sometimes known as the common porpoise or puffing pig on account of its sneeze-like blow when it surfaces to breathe, the illustrated harbour porpoise is not as easily seen as some of its relations. It does not readily 'bow-ride' in front of sea-going craft and shows little of itself at the surface. Observers who therefore get prolonged views of it are particularly fortunate and a fleeting glimpse is more usual.

Porpoises have four collective nouns associated with them (which they share with whales). Those better known include *school* and *pod*, whilst the term *herd* is in keeping with other semantic bovine connections such as cow, bull and calf for the female, male and young respectively. The word *gam*, as well as being another collective noun for porpoises and whales, has a definition as a social gathering of whalers at sea. Generally speaking, the term *pod* is used for smaller, perhaps family, groups whilst *school* or *herd* refers to the larger groups.

The collective noun *pod* is also applied to hippopotamus, seals, and whiting; *school* to fish and *herd* to many creatures, but those specifically listed as herds include wrens, curlew, antelopes, asses, chamois, elephants, giraffe, goats, hares, seals and sperm whales.

Porpoises, like most cetaceans, have suffered in recent times from human interference. This has been both directly in terms of hunting and also indirectly from habitat pollution and degradation, as well as accidental capture in fishing nets. Nevertheless, the harbour porpoise is still the commonest and most widely-distributed cetacean in British waters.

Grist of bees

Bees have no less than eight collective nouns applied to them. Most people will be familiar with hive, which refers also to the place in which bees live, and **swarm** which is also a verb relating to the mass movement of bees flying to form a new colony. **Colony** itself is another term regularly used not only for bees but also for other creatures living together in a community. The collective noun **cluster**, which means a bunch, is aptly applied to bees specifically which are packed around a queen. The term **drift** is an archaic word for drove meaning a horde, and is applied to swarming bees. The *Oxford Reference Dictionary* lists the word **bike**, which *Chambers Dictionary* defines as 'a nest of wasps, wild bees etc.' It gives the alternative spelling **byke**, but apart from the suggestion that it is a Scottish term, the origins of it are unknown.

The collective noun **grist** seems to be a genuine, if fairly recent term applied to bees, appearing first in print around 1930. In addition to the word's definition as corn for grinding, it is an old American term meaning a portion or quantity, so would appear to have some validity as a collective noun. By far the most obscure collective noun for bees, however, is the term **erst**. This seems only to appear in the AA *Book of the British Countryside* and may be simply a modem example of miscopying (grist?) more evident in earlier mediaeval hand-written manuscripts.

Although when one mentions bees many people think of the honey bee and the complex social structure of the hive, only very few of the thousands of different bee species are in fact social. Most of them are indeed known as 'solitary insects' and have much the same sort of life history as other insect species.

# **H**erd of curlew

The haunting, liquid call of the curlew is synonymous with the winter foreshore and marsh. It is as well known to the farmer, however, as it is to the wildfowler, and anyone who has seen groups of this bird, the largest British wader, on meadows or fields, will readily understand the collective noun *herd.*

The term can be traced as far back as any collective noun, appearing in *The Book of St Albans* in the fifteenth century. At that time, curlews were regularly eaten (along with many other birds which we would not think of eating today!). The idea of curlews providing a source of meat lends even more credence to the term *herd*.

Although not unique, the long slender bill of the curlew, used for probing into soft ground for its invertebrate food, is distinctive. The mottled brown plumage, its protection as a ground-nesting bird, is darker in the summer than in the winter. The curlew's name represents the sound of its call.

Solitary curlews are commonly seen, but they are also often gregarious. Flocks can sometimes consist of several thousand birds at non-breeding times, but even during the breeding season, groups of mature birds will sometimes associate with each other for feeding and roosting.

# over of trout

Anyone who has stood on the bank of a river or leaned over a bridge and, having accustomed their eyes to the play of light on the stones of the riverbed, identified the gentle tail-waving which betrays the position of a waiting trout, will identify with this most evocative of collective nouns. The definition in C.E. Hare's *The Language of Sport*, however, is rather less languid an image – it describes the term ***hover*** as an assembly of trout 'waiting on the edge of fast water in great numbers ready to dash at food brought down by the stream.'

A sea trout is sometimes called a *grey fish*, *whitefish*, *whitling*, *square tail*, *sewin*, *black neb* or *black tail*; trout newly emerged from the ova are called *alevin*; young fish of the whole salmon family are called *parr* after their umbilical sac is gone, but young sea-trout are also called *peal* or *herling*.

A *finnock* is a young seatrout which has not yet reached spawning age; a *smolt* is a young salmon or sea trout going to sea for the first time; a sea trout smolt is also called a *sprod* or *yellow fin*; a *grilse* is a fish on its first return from saltwater, sometimes called a *fork-tail*. A *pugg* is a third year fish. A *springer* is a fish returning to the river from the sea in spring and a *kelt*, *kipper* or *slat* is an 'unclean' fish which has not recovered from spawning. A *baggot*, *shedder* or *rawner* is an unspawned fish after the usual spawning time, and a *maiden* is a fish which has never spawned. A large trout is sometimes referred to as an *alderman* and a *banker* is a trout lying up close to a bank. Got all that?

indle of kittens

Cats have six collective nouns which may be applied to them. In addition there are further collectives which apply to specific types of cats e.g. a *pride*, *sault*, *sowse*, *troop* or even *flock* of lions, or a *leap* of leopards. The six collective nouns relating to other cats are the 'true term' *clowder*, the terms *destruction* and *dout* (sometimes wrongly copied as 'dour') which apply just to wild cats, a *cluster* of domestic cats (sometimes appearing as *clutter*), a *glaring* of cats, obviously relating to the cats' eyes at night, and finally a *kindle* (sometimes written as *kinder*), a term which applies to young cats or kittens. All of these nouns have very early references in mediaeval literature, the most recent being the reference for *kindle* in *The Book of St Albans* of 1486. This term is also applied to young rabbits and hares.

Cats were probably first domesticated in the Middle East before the year 3,000 BC and there are now some fifty million of them in western European homes alone. They have been worshipped as gods, regarded as good-luck charms, as agents of witches and the devil, as well as being loved as household companions.

The British wildcat, looking rather like a largish tabby but with a much bushier tale, was once to be found all over Scotland, England and Wales. However, by the beginning of this century it seemed to be close to extinction, confined to just a small area of Scotland. Having subsequently enjoyed some increase in range and numbers, the figures today relating to wildcats (as opposed to those including hybrids with domestic cats) are perilously low. The wildcat's Latin name *felis sylvestris*, meaning cat of the woods, makes it the original 'Sylvester'.

nob of waterfowl

Other birds could replace the moorhens in this illustration, as the term **knob** can refer to many species. Indeed it may refer to groups of varied wildfowl or waterfowl (wildfowl usually meaning ducks, geese or swans; waterfowl usually being a wider, more vague term for freshwater aquatic birds), or particular individual species. Different books and authors identify a **knob** of pochard, widgeon or teal. In addition, some authorities stipulate that a **knob** must be less than thirty birds. A little **knob** has been described as being between ten and twenty birds.

If there are more than thirty wildfowl, some say, the terms **bunch**, **trip**, **plump**, **sord** or **sute** should be used, but this is by no means a universal opinion. Furthermore, **rush** is an alternative collective noun for pochard, **company** for widgeon and **spring** an alternative for teal. Just one reference has been made to a **coil** of teal and in the air, widgeon and others are referred to as a **flight**. Make sure you get the correct word the next time you're feeding the ducks!

It would seem that the term **knob** is a relatively recent one. It appeared in *The Complete Crossword Reference Book* by C. Thorn in 1932, and in *Nuttal's Dictionary* a few years earlier, but not apparently before that. In contrast a **sprynge** of teal appears in Egerton's manuscript of 1452, whilst the terms **rush**, **trip**, **flight** and **company** have certainly been around since H.C. Folkard's *The Wildfowler* in 1859.

The moorhens illustrated are common birds of lakes, ponds, canals and rivers. Breeding birds are fiercely territorial and prefer their own company. At other times, particularly in hard weather, flocks of up to forty birds will group together.

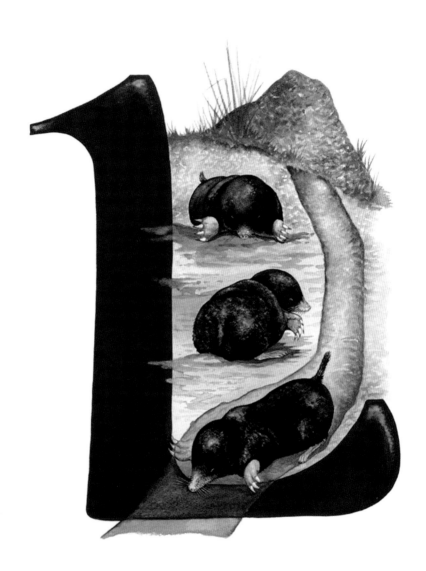

abour of moles

Another evocative collective noun, a ***labour*** of moles conjures up images of the hardworking miners toiling underground for the common good. Moles seem always to have been regarded as industrious. In the seventeenth century, John Dryden translated Virgil:

> *The field-mouse builds her garner underground,*
> *For gather'd grain the blind laborious mole*
> *In winding mazes works her hidden hole.*

The moles' industry is often evident above ground where the characteristic molehills indicate the activity below. Not always a welcome sight to farmers, the mole has long been regarded as vermin. In days gone by, specialist molecatchers were a common feature of rural life. Not only did they kill moles for the farmer, the fur was in demand for two reasons – clothing and plumbing! The velvety, short, stiff fur of the mole is unusual in that it has no natural grain. It stands straight up, allowing the mole to move forwards or backwards in its confined burrow without ruffling its fur. It is also very dense to prevent fouling from soil or dirt. These qualities made the pelt of the mole attractive as a clothing material – particularly for moleskin breeches. Plumbers at one time also valued a moleskin to wipe smooth the tapered solder joint between two pieces of lead pipe.

An alternative collective noun for moles is ***company***.

oomery of guillemots

There are three species of guillemot which congregate around British shores. The scarcest of the three is an Arctic bird, Brunnich's guillemot. It is only an occasional winter visitor to this country but its Latin name, *Uria lomvia*, may well have given rise to the collective noun ***loomery***. Another more plausible possibility is that it derives from the northern dialect term for the bird, 'loom'. The term applies strictly to a nesting colony of guillemots.

The common guillemot and the black guillemot make up the three species. They are members of the auk family and are birds of the sea and coast. Guillemots are very sociable birds and it would seem therefore most appropriate that they have a company term, and yet the guillemot is missing from many lists of collective nouns. Certainly the guillemot is not traditional sporting quarry and did not therefore appear in many of the earlier sporting books.

Loomery is only one of two terms recorded for guillemots. The other is ***bazaar***, which could well relate to the hustle and bustle of the nesting colony of guillemots, which resembles the thronging crowds of a busy market. Every available space is taken up on suitable cliff nesting sites, with noisy nesting birds competing for the best location and bringing up their young surrounded by others of their kind.

The guillemot has perhaps the biggest colour variation in its eggs of any British bird. Although consistently pyriform (pear-shaped), eggs have different base colours with further different coloured spots, lines, streaks and blotches.

urmuration of starlings

The company term ***murmuration*** appeared as ***murmuracyon*** in the fifteenth-century Egerton manuscript. It is hardly surprising that this collective noun is long-established; such sociable birds have always been associated with our towns and cities.

An equally old and established term is a ***chattering*** of starlings. Both collective nouns are intended to convey something of the noise which these garrulous birds make when they assemble in huge numbers for their winter roosts. Starling populations are not as healthy as they once were. Recent declines resonate with the serious decline at the beginning of the nineteenth century from which they were at one time recovered.

Chattering also appeared in the Egerton manuscript as a company term for choughs, although this has been regarded as a misspelling of the more accepted term for choughs: ***clattering***. A young starling is called a *stare* (also an Irish name for the adult birds), and this term is also one of the company terms used for owls.

The starling has beautiful plumage which changes with the seasons. Its beauty often goes unrecognised owing to our familiarity with the species. T.A. Coward called the starling an 'avian humourist', and indeed the bird has comical attributes. The male, perched perhaps on top of a chimney pot, may be heard not only to chuckle and chatter, but also on occasions to make the liquid call of the curlew. A great mimic, the starling can repeat a variety of different sounds, and not just those necessarily made by other birds. Even machines like garden mowers can be imitated!

ustering of Storks

The collective noun ***mustering*** is unsurprisingly derived from the word muster, meaning a general gathering or assembly. Mustering is applied particularly to troops who are arranged together for an inspection or a particular task. In the animal world, muster is also a round-up of livestock (acting as both the noun and the verb), particularly in the Antipodes.

Chambers Dictionary lists ***muster*** as a collective noun also for peacocks. The development of ***muster*** to ***mustering*** can be seen as a minor evolution when compared to many of the other corruptions identified for other collectives. James Lipton's authoritative book *An Exaltation of Larks* lists and illustrates a ***mustering*** of storks but with no explanatory text and certainly it is a common feature of many other published lists.

There are many different types of stork around the world. The illustrated White Stork is a summer migrant to Europe. It arrives in early spring, approximately nine months after mid-summer's day. In days gone by, this was a much more significant festival of merrymaking and drinking than it is today. Perhaps the arrival of numerous babies resulting from the summer revelry, at about the same time as the storks arrived back from their wintering grounds, gave rise to the folk-lore of the stork dropping the babies down the chimney from their beaks! Another reported theory of Scandinavian folk-lore tells how new babies' souls came from the pool where the storks fed. The storks brought them in their beaks to the new mother. Whatever the truth, the phenomenon was popularised in the tales of Hans Christian Andersen and is now a common feature of children's books.

ute of hounds

Hounds, in keeping with other birds and animals associated with hunting, have a number of different collective nouns. A *leash* is a set of three hounds, especially greyhounds; a *couple* is a term for a brace of hunting dogs usually applied when they are running, while the word *brace* is itself another legitimate collective noun. Some authorities maintain that terminology for hounds generally should be differentiated from greyhounds specifically: two greyhounds a *brace*, two hounds a *couple*: three greyhounds a *leash*, three hounds a *couple and a half*.

The more general terms for an unspecified number of hounds include *pack* and *mute* (from Old French *meute* meaning pack or kennel, rather than any reference to a lack of vocalisation). The word *kennel* itself is a genuine noun of assembly for hounds as well as a place in which dogs live. *Kennel* is also the correct collective noun for dogs other than hounds. A *hunt* is both a group of hounds and a group of huntsmen, as well of course as the chase itself. A limited number of sources quote further collective nouns for a group of hounds as *cry* or *stable*. The term *litter* is used for a group of whelps or puppies.

A hound is defined as a dog of a kind used in hunting. A *sute* is a further collective noun for these dogs, although it has been quoted in some sources as a term just for bloodhounds. It comes from the word *suite* meaning a train of followers or attenders. A *rache* is a further sub-division of hounds meaning a hound which hunts by scent. C.E. Hare suggests that, along with *pack*, the term *kennel* should be used specifically for raches.

est of mice

There are four species of mice in Britain. They are bright, inquisitive and successful little creatures; the illustrated house mouse, for example, is found world-wide. It is not indigenous to Britain, though, and may have been the first mammal to have been introduced through human activity. Evidence shows that this mouse was certainly present in this country during the Iron Age, and it has always co-existed with humans. It steals our food, makes a home in our houses and keeps one genetic step ahead by developing immunities to many rodent poisons intended to bring about its downfall.

The most widespread and abundant mouse in Britain, however, is the woodmouse. Also known as the long-tailed field mouse, it is not as dependent on woodland as its name implies, being adaptable to many habitats. Indeed, it will readily follow the example of the house mouse and come into our homes during times of hard weather.

The yellow-necked mouse looks like a large woodmouse, which it was once considered to be. It is now regarded as a distinct species.

The harvest mouse is the smallest British mouse and perhaps the most appealing of the whole family. They live in meadows and hedgerows. The development of modem farming practices meant that the harvest mouse was in danger of becoming a great rarity, but it has clung on and is now even re-colonising lost ground.

ye of pheasants

Pheasants are not indigenous British birds. They initially came from Asia, but were successfully introduced to many parts of Europe and North America. There are many different species of pheasant, and even those which are now regarded as wild in Britain take different forms. These latter birds originate from many different types which include the common pheasant (with no white collar) from Armenia, the Chinese ring-necked pheasant (with incomplete white collar) from Eastern China and Pallas's pheasant (which has a complete broad white collar) from Manchuria. All forms have freely interbred producing a wide variety of birds with collars in varying degrees of white.

Legend has it that the pheasant was introduced to Europe by Jason and the Argonauts. The exact time of its introduction to Britain is disputed. Until recent times, it was assumed that the Romans brought the bird here, but archaeological evidence seems now unable to prove this. Certainly there is documentary evidence of the pheasant being in Britain before the twelfth century. What is not disputed is the pheasant's reputation as a game bird, and it has always been reared as such. Its beautiful plumage is matched by its flavour and suitability for the table.

There are many variations in the spelling of the collective noun, including *nide*, *nie* and *ny*. The word means a hatch or nest of pheasants and relates specifically to the young. C.E. Hare maintains that 'a *nye*' should be 'an eye', arguing that *eye* is the Old English word signifying a brood. It has also been maintained that the word is derived from the French word *nid* meaning nest. Other company terms are *brood* for a family of pheasants, *bouquet* as a general gathering and *brace* for a pair of shot birds.

# **P**ack of stoats

Kenneth Graham's classic children's novel *Wind In The Willows* reinforced the image of stoats and weasels as the arch-villains of the countryside: *'.. a company of skirmishing stoats who stuck at nothing occupied the conservatory'*. Stoats, weasels and ferrets had occupied Toad Hall and the public, it seems, has never forgiven them.

The collective noun itself conjures up images of bullying gangs, but the often-reported marauding ***packs*** of stoats are much more likely simply to have been family groups – there can be up to twelve young in a litter. Their lithe, almost snake-like bodies enable them to follow their prey down holes and burrows, and their sharp teeth and dark eyes complete the picture.

The folklore myth of them sucking blood in vampire-fashion springs from their occasional killing method. Usually they kill with a bite to the back of the neck, but sometimes they will bite the throat of a rabbit and its death is not always instantaneous. Letting go would allow the rabbit to kick out, so injuring the stoat. It holds on, often getting blood on its face and coat in the process. The impressionable observer insists they have seen the stoat sucking the blood of another wild creature!

The stoat's black tail-tip distinguishes it from the weasel. To tell the two apart, it is no use relying on the old joke – 'stoats are stoatally different while weasels are weasily distinguished'! The term ***pack*** is also applied to weasels, wolves, dogs and a predator of freshwater – the perch.

arliament of owls

Owls have always held a special place in our hearts. Their faces, with their large forward-facing eyes, have almost human characteristics. Their nocturnal habits, silent flight and haunting calls have at the same time lent owls a certain mystery. Owls have been identified with wisdom and sagacity; the wise old owl in the gnarled oak is a popular image from children's literature.

There are about 130 species of owl in the world. Six of them have nested regularly in the British Isles. The owls illustrated are tawny owls, also called brown or wood owls. It is *their* call, often wrongly quoted as *too-whit-too-whoo* (this representation combines both male and female calls) which has come to symbolise the call of all owls, even though the call of many bears no resemblance. Numerous ghost stories have their origins in, for example, the chilling shriek of a barn owl flying over some rural graveyard!

The term ***parliament*** is not included in many early lists as a collective noun for owls, and yet its definition as a group of owls appears in present-day dictionaries. This is in contrast to other terms which have no current dictionary reference, yet are well documented from the early books. ***Parliament*** appears more often as a company term for *rooks*. Groups of owls have also been referred to as a ***stare*** of owls (***stare*** being in addition a term for a young starling). The medieval poet Geoffrey Chaucer wrote the *Parlement of Foules* which culminates in a large gathering of different birds all trying to find a mate.

All of our resident owls except one are typically to be found as individuals or in pairs. The exception is the long-eared owl which can be found in communal roosts during winter to form a true ***parliament*** of owls.

arty of jays

The jay is the most colourful member of the crow family. Often shot as vermin, it is loud and raucous, the hooligan of the woodland in which it lives. One is far more likely to hear the harsh screaming of the jay than to see the bird, despite its distinctive chestnut flanks, white rump and blue wing-flashes. Its retiring habit and love of the treetops means that only sharp-eyed observers will regularly see it.

Jays are especially fond of beech mast and acorns; indeed, they have been said to play a significant part in oak tree propagation through their habit of food-hoarding.

Jays are not as sociable as some other members of the crow family, for example their relative the rook. Jays tend to become territorial in the breeding season, when even non-breeding birds will not be tolerated. At other times, however, jays will often form groups which may be especially large if the acorn crop fails and food is scarce.

There are two recorded collective nouns. ***Party*** is the less well-known, the other being ***band***. This latter term was perhaps first quoted in the American *Pacific Sportsman* magazine of 1929, and indeed now appears in most lists. A ***party*** of jays is certainly referred to in the 1967 book of collective nouns by B. Wildsmith, called simply *Birds*.

od of whales

Pod is one of five collective nouns listed for whales. It is usually the one applied to smaller numbers of whales such as those making up a family group. The term is also referenced for hippopotamus, seals and whiting particularly, but *Chambers Dictionary*, following its definition of *pod* as a *school*, goes on to say it is sometimes used for other groups of animals, fish and birds. Interestingly, the term *herd* is listed for sperm whales only and the *Oxford Reference Dictionary* includes the word *grind* as a noun of assembly exclusively for bottle-nosed whales. In addition to *school*, the other collective noun for whales is *gam* (see *Gam of Porpoises*).

Whales in recent times have captured the spirit of the modem conservation movement. Part of the reason for the public condemnation of whale hunting was not only the wish to protect the whale for its own sake, but also the growing realisation that the whale's intelligence was of a high enough order to render the killing methods unacceptable. Whales, like so many of the world's creatures, are not completely safe yet and there are still those nations which wish to hunt them, but they have gained significant protection - enough to allow for some optimism about their future. Great therapeutic benefit is claimed from time spent watching these gentle giants of the deep.

The illustrated killer whales, one of the toothed whale species and usually classified as dolphins, are fairly common and regularly seen in the seas around the northern British coast. The minke whale is the only baleen whale commonly seen in British waters. The commonest whale species to be found around Britain is the long-finned pilot whale, whilst the northern bottlenose whale and the sperm whale are rare sightings in deep waters.

Quantity of smelts

This rather mundane collective noun is one of a fair number which are applied exclusively to fish. Its reported origin is just as ordinary as the word itself: Isaac Walton, in his classic *The Compleat Angler* of 1676 refers to 'vast *quantities*' of smelts coming up the River Thames in such numbers that even women and children began angling for them! The term subsequently stuck and appeared in later lists.

The origin of the smelt's name is rather more colourful. It is said that the name derives from the opinion of some that the body of the smelt bears the scent of violets. Whilst others have declared that the smell of the fish is that of cucumbers (an opinion supported by contemporary field guides), the principle of the smelt's natural aroma having influenced its name remains the same!

Although not members of the salmon family, smelts are salmon-like in a number of respects. They have, like salmon and trout, an adipose fin - a small fatty fin lacking rays which is situated between the tail and dorsal fin. Also like salmon and sea trout, smelts are anadromous, that is they return to spawn in freshwater rivers having spent their growing years in the sea. They do this in Spring, returning to the sea again after a few weeks or months to repeat the process again the following year. Sexually mature usually at the age of two to three years, they may spawn each year until they are fifteen years old.

aft of duck

There are many company terms for wildfowl in general and ducks in particular. ***Raft*** is not one that has references in the very earliest of sources, but is currently accepted as a term for ducks on water. Such ducks have also been referred to as a ***paddling*** or a ***bunch*** of ducks. When in flight ducks are referred to as a ***team***. Terms which seem not to be specific about the ducks' position include a ***trip***, ***plump*** and a ***knob*** or ***little knob*** of duck. Groups of pochard particularly are known as a ***rush*** or a ***diving***.

The onomatopoeic term ***dopping*** is applied solely to sheldrakes, although seemingly could be applied to all shelducks. The term is said to derive from their habit of disappearing suddenly under water if disturbed, making a ***dopping*** noise. (A short bobbing curtsey was known as a dop in East Anglia, so this may also have been an influence.)

The number of different collective nouns springs not only from the fact that ducks have always been a popular and largely accessible sporting quarry. Nor is it just to do with the large number of duck species which frequent both salt and freshwater habitats around Britain. It may also be because, unlike many other quarry species, particularly game birds, ducks will often be referred to simply by the generic term ***duck***. This can give rise to confusion, and is reflected in company terms which sometimes are used for ducks generally, and at other times for particular individual species.

The ducks illustrated are long-tailed ducks. These are sea ducks which have different summer and winter plumages and are to be found around the northern coasts of Britain outside the breeding season.

ichesse of martens

The illustrated pine marten is the only marten native to Britain. It is a member of the large mustelid family which includes the otter, badger, weasel and polecat. Mustelids get their name from their habit of expelling supposedly musty-smelling secretions from scent glands under the tail. However, the scent of a pine marten is not unpleasant and its Old English name of 'sweetmart' distinguishes it from its more evil-smelling relative – the 'foulmart' or polecat.

The pine marten has a luxuriantly dense, rich chocolate brown coat with a characteristic creamy yellow throat bib. Consequently its fur was prized by royalty and nobles as a trimming for robes of state. Where once the pine marten was widespread across the tree-covered English landscape, it is now confined to a small area of Wales, Scotland and parts of Ireland.

Whilst generally shy, retiring and active mainly at night or at dawn and dusk, shunning human presence, they are known to come regularly to food in certain gardens (they have a special liking for strawberry-jam sandwiches!) and can be induced to take food even from the hand. I have seen a family group in a back yard during broad daylight, feeding on sandwiches right next to a window quite unconcernedly observing the watcher record them on video!

The collective noun is still sometimes written *richesse* in the same way as it appeared in print in mediaeval literature. The modem equivalent is *richness*. The term derives from the pine marten's rich fur. It has been incorrectly applied to the bird 'martin' rather than to the animal 'marten'.

Sedge of bitterns

Bitterns share their two collective nouns, many of their habits and much of their own limited habitat with herons. It is regrettable, therefore, that they do not also share their fortunes. For the bittern is now an extremely rare bird in Britain with fewer than 100 breeding males. This is due primarily to the drainage and destruction of their reedbed home, but egg collectors and hunters have also contributed to its downward trend; indeed it became extinct as a breeding species towards the end of the last century, re-establishing itself from migrant flocks to peak in the 1950s before another decline.

Its coloration gives this wading bird perfect camouflage in its dense reedbed habitat; it can also elongate its neck and body at times of danger to further blend into its surroundings. These factors, together with its natural skulking manner, make the bittern one of the most elusive of birds. Paradoxically, the patient observer may on occasions be fortunate enough to witness quite spectacular displays of behaviour, especially during the breeding season, and at other times, when birds may climb precariously and noisily to the tops of reeds with apparent disregard for caution!

The background to collective nouns for bitterns is similar to that for herons, the term **sege** first being recorded in the fifteenth century and subsequently interpreted as **siege**. In 1688 Randle Holme's book *The Academy of Armory and Blazon* not only misspelt **shegh** of herons, but also **seigh** of bitters (sic). Many lists today give both *sedge* and *siege* as company terms for both herons and bitterns, but **sedge** would seem to be more suitable for the bittern, reflecting its more specific habitat.

iege of herons

Herons are represented in Britain by the grey heron. These long-legged, long-necked birds of the waterside, rather incongruously nest together in large trees. At other times they stalk the margins of waterways for their prey of fish, frogs and small mammals. They appear in the very early lists of hunting books owing to the fact that they were once a popular quarry for falconers, *heron-hawking* being a favourite sport.

Herons have at times been given two collective nouns: **siege** and **sedge**. They share both with the bittern, a bird with whom they also share a variety of habits. The company term was originally recorded in a mid-fifteenth-century manuscript and subsequently in *The Book of St Albans* in 1486 as **sege**. This was interpreted in turn as **siege**. A misspelling appeared as a **shegh** of herons in the 1688 book *The Academy of Armory and Blazon* by Randle Holme. Then in 1859 in a book by H.C. Folkard entitled *The Wildfowler*, the term was recorded as **sedge**. While most contemporary lists adhere to the original interpretation, some do quote the latter and some both.

The term **siege** has been recognised as relating to the patient way in which a heron will wait for its prey, just as an army will patiently wait for the surrender of the enemy under siege. The company term should not be confused with the name for the *place* where herons breed, i.e. a *heronry*.

Although it is most usual to see a solitary heron, they can also be sociable outside the breeding season. They will often feed in close proximity to each other, especially on coastlines during winter.

# **S**muck of jellyfish

Appearing in different lists as *smuck*, *smack* or *stuck*, it seems likely that the collective nouns for jellyfish are all derived from the original printed version *smuck* contained in *Nuttall's Dictionary* of the 1920s. *Nuttall's Dictionary* itself defined the term as 'a *crowd* of jellyfish', but whereas *smuck* and its derivatives found themselves in a number of subsequent lists – *crowd* did not appear again.

There is no record of how the terms originated. A smack is a small-decked fishing vessel in which there is a well for keeping live fish. It is unlikely, however, that jellyfish would have been kept in one. I like to think that the term's origin may rather have been onomatopoeic: something to do with the noise made when one inadvertently steps upon a stranded jellyfish on the beach, or perhaps the sound made when one might prod and lift it with a stick and part-suck its body like a plastic bag full of water from the wet sand – smmmuck! like a noisy kiss.

Whatever its origins, it is appropriate for there to be a collective noun for jellyfish: they are often to be seen drifting with the water currents in large groups. Often, many can be seen stranded on the beach together, where they dry out and die.

The Common Jellyfish generally feeds on plankton, but larger jellyfish such as the illustrated Lion's Mane Jellyfish and the Compass Jellyfish feed on small fish and other animals which they trap with their stinging tentacles. Paradoxically, certain fish such as the whiting, which seem to be immune to the stings, take shelter and refuge amongst the tentacles.

 ounder of Boar

The word boar, as well as being a noun for the male pig, has become over time the accepted term for wild pigs. It was the Egerton Manuscript of 1452 that first recorded the collective noun as a *singular* of boar, with later authorities adding the term *sounder*, which became the more popular. The word *singular* certainly seems odd for a collective noun. C.E. Hare suggests that even though it appears in many lists it is indeed a mistake, quoting the *Book of St Albans* as confirming its application instead for a single boar of four years or older – the true company term is *sounder*.

C.E. Hare is also specific about the distinctive nature of collective nouns for tame and wild swine (swine simply being a synonym for pigs): wild swine are a *sounder*, tame swine a *drift*, *trip*, *doylt*, or *herd*. He still lists *sounder* or *singular* for boar specifically.

The wild boar was hunted to extinction in Great Britain during the thirteenth century. Later re-introduced by James I, these animals too all met their end at the hands (or rather the lances) of the hunters.

However, animals have escaped from farms in recent times and boar now roam wild across significant areas of the British countryside, including Dartmoor, Kent, Sussex, Herefordshire and Gloucestershire. Indeed, such has been their breeding success that a controversial cull has recently been proposed. Many householders near to the Forest of Dean would be supportive – they have had their lawns and gardens completely destroyed by the rooting behaviour of these animals. Ironically however, it is this very behaviour that is one of the arguments in the boars' favour; turning over the ground like this in its typical woodland haunt is reported to be good for the ecosystem.

warm of eels

At first sight an unlikely collective noun for eels, the term *swarm* was first recorded in a book entitled *Rural Sports*, written in 1801 by Reverend W.B. Daniel. This became a standard work for hunting, fishing and shooting terms and therefore has some integrity. The term has subsequently been included in many lists. One of the dictionary definitions for *swarm* is a throng of small animals, particularly on the move. On reflection, therefore, it is a particularly appropriate noun of assembly for the young elvers which travel in their multitudes back to their freshwater homes.

The life cycle of the eel is now well researched and is one of those amazing stories which would seem to belong more in the world of fiction than fact. Eels spend up to nineteen years growing from immature yearlings in fresh waters of all types across Europe. They are known as 'yellow eels' because of their brownish yellow colour. Ultimately changing colour to black and silver, the adults, known as 'silver eels', make the journey of up to 7,000 kilometres back to the Sargasso Sea where they were born. The adults die after spawning in the spring, leaving the small, transparent 'glass eels' to make their way back with the help of the Gulf Stream and the North Atlantic Drift to the freshwater homes of their parents. This journey is now thought to take about one year, when the whole amazing process begins again.

An old country superstition was that to put a live eel in a heavy drinker's glass of beer would cure him of his vice. It would certainly have put him off that particular drink!

# **Trip of dotterel**

A dotterel is a dullard or a stupid person; the bird of the same name is so called because of its supposed foolishness in letting itself be easily caught, and indeed the second part of the bird's Latin name *Eudromias morinellus* means 'little fool'. The name given to it in Norfolk of stone runner, after its habit of alighting on rocky outcrops, seems a kinder term for this delightful wading bird.

A member of the plover family, the dotterel was once prized for its flesh, and seemingly did allow itself to be taken too easily, for it is now scarce. Dotterel have been described as being fearless at their nests and very tame and approachable when travelling.

Dotterel in Britain are summer visitors or passage migrants to their remote mountain-top breeding grounds. Birds do still breed in Scotland and parts of northern England, but they are mainly seen towards the end of April and the beginning of May in small parties or *trips*. Although their breeding plumage may appear distinctive (only males are illustrated), dotterel can be very difficult to see on the ground.

The word *trip* is an accepted collective noun and one which is also applied to goats – and hares *(see overleaf)*. It is well established and was first recorded in Osbaliston's book *British Sportsmen* in 1785. Although the bird itself may be obscure to anyone not involved with ornithology, the term *trip* is surprisingly consistent in turning up in most lists of company terms. This may well be because the bird was at one time much more commonly known, owing to the fact that it was regularly eaten.

rip of hares

A traditional quarry species, the hare has nine associated collective nouns. This large number is in keeping with other birds and animals which are either used in hunting or else are themselves the hunted. Two of the nine are regarded as 'true company terms'. The first is ***trip***, a term also applied to goats, sheep, pigs and dotterel. The second is ***drove***, and may have been applied to hares because of the way in which they were driven during the hunt.

The term ***husk*** is apparently an old name for a company of hares, whilst a ***trace*** of hares refers to its footprint in snow. Regarding the origin of a ***down*** of hares, it is thought that different spellings such as ***downe***, ***dunne***, and ***dun*** may point to a comparison with the word 'donie', an old country name for the hare. In his book *Language of Sport*, C.E. Hare (who I understand has no family connection to this animal), writes that the term herd is a miscopying from a 'herd of hartes'. In common with other animals of the hunt, the hare shares the collective nouns ***brace*** when referring to groups of two, and ***leash*** for groups of three individuals. The term ***kindle*** refers just to young hares.

There are two types of hare in Britain: the Common or European Hare (illustrated) and the Mountain Hare. Much folklore surrounds the hare. For example it was believed if one was seen by a pregnant woman, she would give birth to a baby with a hare-lip. Witches were once believed to turn into hares which then stole cows' milk, and the witches' familiar, the black cat, was the hare in earlier times.

nkindness of ravens

One of the most powerful birds of legend, the raven is steeped in mythology and antiquity. The word *raven* itself has changed little from the Anglo-Saxon *hrafn*. Odin, the great Norse God of War, Victories and Death was also the Raven God. His two pet ravens would fly far and wide before alighting on his shoulder to whisper news to him. Ravens live to a considerable age and have been known to repeat words in captivity. The tame ravens are a feature of the Tower of London and it is said that if ever the ravens should disappear from the Tower, the monarchy will come to an end.

The explanation of the collective noun is no less strange. It was thought long ago that the breeding ravens gave no parental care to their chicks. People imagined that they expelled the young from the nest, leaving them to fend for themselves until they saw that they were the colour they ought to be. If they were indeed a glossy black they were cared for. It was said that such **unkindness** was repaid by the youngsters, however, for when the parents were old and their beaks worn, their offspring would offer no help. The group term was referred to in the Egerton manuscript of 1452.

In their mountainous, or coastal cliff home, ravens do in fact display a perceived **unkindness**. They will often not tolerate other birds near them, and although they scavenge, they will also kill small birds (often in the nest) and mammals with their massive bill.

Ravens often occur in quite large flocks consisting of immature birds and adults which do not hold territories.

olery of birds

Unlike most other collective nouns in this book, the term ***volery*** applies to a number of birds generally rather than to one particular species. There are a number of company terms for birds which fall into this category. The most common term for an assemblage of birds is ***flock***, but other alternatives include ***congregation***, ***aviary***, ***multitude***, ***host***, on the water a ***raft***, and the collective which is applied just to *small* birds, ***dissimulation***. The word ***brood*** is often used for the nestlings, chicks or young hatched from a *clutch* or *set* of eggs.

Birds which breed together in large groups are said to form a ***colony***. A male and female bird together are referred to as a ***pair*** and two dead birds (usually game birds) are called a ***brace***. The collective noun which comes closest to being a direct substitute for ***volery***, however, is ***flight***. Indeed, some artistic licence has been exercised in the illustration, for according to C.E. Hare a true ***volery*** of birds ought to be in flight. The term ***volery*** first appeared in the Special *Daily Mail* Edition of *Nuttal's Dictionary*.

Other terms referring to flying birds specifically include a ***wedge*** of swans, an ***exaltation*** of larks and a ***skein*** of geese, while the term ***flight*** can refer to birds generally but also in particular to doves, dunlin, goshawks, larks, pigeons, plovers, pochard, swallows, widgeon, or woodcock!

A little owl is illustrated in the centre of the picture and clockwise around it from the top left are: a male pied flycatcher, a male white wagtail, a male bullfinch and a pair of long-tailed tits.

Warren of rabbits

This particular collective noun appears in just one list known to the author and yet its use as a company term is endorsed by the definition in *Chambers Dictionary*. This is in contrast to other more generally accepted collective nouns which appear in many lists but often have no contemporary dictionary references. Certainly the word *warren* is more commonly known as a series of interconnected rabbit burrows. *Colony* is also listed as a collective noun for rabbits, with the terms *kindle* and *nest* applied to their young.

The term 'rabbit' itself only referred to young animals until the eighteenth century, an adult being called a cony (or coney). Nevertheless it still seems surprising that lists of collective nouns often contain separate references for both. This is a tradition going back to the very earliest mediaeval manuscripts, where for example the Egerton manuscript lists the company term for conies as *bery*, now written *bury*, along with a listing for *neste* of rabbits. C.E. Hare suggests that as a corruption of 'burrow' the term *bury* is properly the name of the conies' home and should not be regarded as a legitimate collective noun. Such an argument does not sit easily, however, with the definitions of *warren* above. Two conies are a *couple*; three a *couple and a half*. Many conies together have been termed a *fayre game* or simply a *game* of conies.

Rabbits share many of the country superstitions related to hares. To carry a rabbit's foot is thought to bring good luck. Good luck can also be achieved by saying 'rabbits' three times on the first day of the month, although the charm loses its potency if it is not the first thing uttered early in the morning!

Wisp of snipe

The common snipe is a resident British wading bird whose numbers are significantly increased by winter visitors. It is also called the full or whole snipe which distinguishes it from the smaller jack snipe. It is a heavily streaked and patterned bird which means it is well camouflaged amongst the vegetation of the flooded fields and marshes which it frequents.

If the snipe is disturbed it flies with a rapid, low zigzag flight, then often rises high into the air. This distinctive, dodging flight has no doubt saved many an individual from the table, as it is a prized sporting quarry. Another distinctive feature of the snipe in the air is its ability to 'drum' its outer tail feathers in its territorial diving flights.

The snipe is generally, though not strictly, gregarious and has two group terms. The fifteenth century Egerton manuscript first makes reference to a *walke* of snipe, a term repeated in *The Book of St Albans* and subsequently appearing as *walk* in many modern lists. The term is thought to refer to the snipe's characteristic method of movement! Chambers' Dictionary lists the same term for a flock of wagtails.

In 1785 Osbaldiston's dictionary-style book *British Sportsmen* listed the group term for snipe as a *wisp* or *whisp*. This is thought to refer to the fine, light zigzag flight of the bird, and appears equally often in subsequent lists. Indeed, this term is one of relatively few which have regular contemporary usage. Dead birds have been referred to as a *couple* or a *leash* of snipe.

# oke of oxen

The dictionary definition of ox is 'a general name for the male or female of common domestic cattle'. The term, however, applies particularly to a castrated male, but has been extended to cover other animals of bovine type. The word oxen is, of course, simply the plural. Although an archaic usage of the term 'cattle' related to horses and sheep, cattle in more recent times has clearly meant cows and bulls, or oxen. And yet, interestingly, lists of collective nouns nearly always differentiate between cattle and oxen. Some have even differentiated between cattle and 'kine', simply a plural word for cows.

The group terms listed for oxen are *yoke*, *team*, *drove* and *herd*. Whereas the term *yoke* clearly relates to just a pair of oxen joined together under a frame of wood (modem dictionaries clearly specify definitions for the group term as well as the common noun), the word *team* is a more flexible number of animals pulling a plough or wagon. It is also applied to horses. A *drove* is a 'true company term' also listed as a collective noun used for asses, cattle, hares, sheep and 'beasts'. Similarly, *herd* is a true company term. It is one of the most widely applied and its *listed* use is shared by antelopes, asses, bucks, buffaloes, cattle, chamois, deer, elephants, giraffes, goats, hares, harts, horses, porpoises, seals, shorthorns, swine, sperm whales and wolves!

Company terms for cattle are listed as *drove*, *herd*, *drift* and the Australian term *mob*. These terms are shared by 'kine' in those lists in which there is a separate entry.

It would be more usual now to see a line of tractors rather than a *yoke* of oxen!

A List of Terms

A

Animals	Menagerie
Antelopes	Cluster, Herd, Tribe
Ants	Colony, Army
Apes	Shrewdness
Asses	Pace, Herd, Drove

B

Baboons	Flange
Badgers	Cete, Colony
Bears	Sloth, Sleuth
Beasts	Drove, Flock
Beaver	Colony
Bees	Cluster, Colony, Erst, Grist, Swarm, Hive, Drift, Bike
Birds	Volery, Congregation, Flock, Assemblage, Flight, Party, Multitude, Horde, Host, Raft, Aviary, Brood
(Small Birds)	Dissimulation
Bitterns	Sedge, Siege
Boars	Singular, Sounder
Bucks	Herd, Brace, Leash
Buffaloes	Herd, Gang

B

Bustards	Flock
Butterflies	Flight

C

Camels	Flock
Capercaillies	Tok
Caterpillars	Army
Cats	Clowder, Cluster, Clutter, Glaring, Dout, Dour, Destruction, Kindle
Cattle	Drove, Herd, Mob, Drift
Chamois	Herd
Chickens	Peep
Choughs	Chattering, Clattering
Clams	Bed
Cockles	Bed
Colts	Rag, Rake
Conies *(see Rabbits)*	Bury, Warren, Fayre Game, Game
Coots	Fleet, Covert
Cormorants	Flight
Coyote	Pack
Cranes	Herd, Sedge, Siege
Crows	Murder
Cubs	Litter
Curlew	Herd
Curs	Cowardice

D

Deer (all species) Herd, Mob, Leash
Dogfish   Troop
Dogs   Kennel, Pack
Donkey   Drove
Dotterel   Trip
Doves   Flight, Dole, Dule,
                Pitying, True Love,
                Piteousness
Ducks   Raft, Bunch, Paddling,
                Badelynge, Team, Sore,
                Safe
Dunlin   Flight

E

Eagles   Convocation
Eels   Swarm
Eland   Herd
Elephants   Herd
Elk   Gang

F

Ferrets   Business
Fieldfares Flock
Finches   Charm, Chirm
Fish   Shoal, Draught, Haul, Run,
                Catch, School, Aquarium,
                Cran, Flock, Leash
Flies   Swarm, Business, Cloud,
                Grist
Fowls   Scry
Foxes   Earth, Skulk, Leash,
                Troop
Frogs   Army, Colony

G

Geese   Gaggle, Skein, Team,
                Wedge, Lag, Flock
Geldings   Brace
Giraffes   Herd, Corps
Gnats   Swarm, Cloud, Horde
Goats   Trip, Herd, Tribe, Trib,
                Flock
Goldfinches Charm, Chirm,
                Trimming, Trembling
Gorillas   Whoop
Grasshoppers Cloud
Grouse   Pack, Covey, Brood
Guillemots Bazaar, Loomery
Gulls   Colony

H

Hares   Drove, Husk, Down, Herd,
                Trace, Trip, Brace, Leash,
                Kindle
Harts   Herd
Hawks   Cast, Leash, Flight, Couple
Hedgehogs   Array
Hens   Brood
Heron   Siege, Sedge
Herrings   Shoal, Glean, Army
Hippos   Pod, Herd
Horses   Harrass, Stable, Herd,
                String, Team, Stud
Hounds   Brace, Couple, Mute,
                Pack, Cry, Stable, Hunt,
                Meet
       (Bloodhounds) Sute
       (Greyhounds) Brace, Leash
       (Raches) Kennel, Pack
Hummingbirds   Charm

I

Impala	Couple
Insects	Swarm, Plague, Flight

J

Jackrabbit	Husk
Jays	Party, Band
Jellyfishes	Smuck, Smack, Stuck

K

Kangaroos	Troop, Mob
Kine	*see* Cattle

L

Lapwing	Deceit, Desert
Larks	Exaltation, Flight, Bevy
Leopards	Leap, Lepe
Lice	Flock
Lions	Sault, Sowse, Pride, Troop, Flock
Locusts	Swarm, Cloud, Plague

M

Magpies	Tiding
Mallard	Sute, Sord, Flush
Mares	Stud
Martens	Richness, Richesse
Mice	Nest
Moles	Labour, Company
Monkeys	Troup, Cartload, Tribe
Moose	Herd
Mules	Barren, Rake, Pack, Span
Mussels	Bed

N

Nightingales	Watch

O

Otters	Family, Bevy
Owls	Stare, Parliament
Oxbirds	Fling
Oxen	Team, Yoke, Drove, Herd
Oysters	Bed, Hive

P

Parrots	Company, Flock
Partridges	Covey
Peacocks	Pride, Muster, Ostentation
Penguins	Rookery, Colony
Perch	Pack
Pheasants	Kit, Nye, Nide, Brood, Bouquet, Brace
Pigeon	Flight, Flock
Pigs	Litter, Drove, Flock, Trip
Plovers	Stand, Wing, Congregation, Flight, Leash
Pochard	Knob, Rush, Flight, Diving, Bunch
Ponies	String
Porpoises	School, Pod, Gam, Herd
Poultry	Run
Ptarmigan	Covey
Pups	Litter

Q

Quail	Bevy, Drift

R

Rabbits   Warren, Nest, Colony,
Kindle
Racehorses   Field, String
Racoons   Nursery
Ravens   Unkindness
Redwing   Crowd
Rhinoceros   Crash
Roebucks/Roes   Bevy
Rooks   Parliament, Building,
Clamour
Ruffs   Hill

S

Salmon   Bind
Sardines   Family
Seals   Herd, Pod, Rookery
Sheep   Flock, Hurtle, Drift,
Mob, Trip, Drove, Down
Sheldrakes   Dopping
Shorthorns   Herd
Smelts   Quantity
Snakes   Bed, Den, Knot
Snipe   Wisp, Walk, Couple,
Leash
Spaniels   Couple
Sparrows   Host, Tribe
Spiders   Cluster, Clutter
Squirrels   Dray, Drey, Colony
Starlings   Murmuration, Chattering
Stoats   Pack
Storks   Mustering
Swallows   Flight
Swans   Game, Herd, Wedge,
Bevy, Tank, Team
Swifts   Flock

Swine **(wild)**   Sounder, Singular
        (tame)   Drift, Trip, Doylt, Herd

T

Teal   Knob, Spring, Bunch, Coil
Thrushes   Mutation
Tigers   Ambush
Toads   Knot, Knob, Nest
Trotters (pigs)   Nest, Set
Trout   Hover
Turkeys   Rafter
Turtles   Bale, Dule

V

Vipers   Nest, Brood

W

Wasps   Nest
Waterfowl   Sute, Bunch, Knob,
Plump
Weasels   Pack
Whales   Pod, Gam, School, Run
  (Bottle-nosed)   Grind
  (Sperm whales)   Herd
Whelps   Litter
Whiting   Pod
Widgeon   Bunch, Trip, Knob, Plump,
Sord, Sute
Wolves   Route, Pack, Herd
Woodcock   Fall, Flight
Woodpeckers   Descent
Wrens   Chime, Herd

Z

Zebra   Herd

Bibliography

AA Book of the British Countryside, Drive Publications, 1973

Animals, Brian Wildsmith, Oxford University Press, 1967

Birds, Brian Wildsmith, Oxford University Press, 1967

The Bird Lover's Weekend Book, Eric Hardy, Seely Service, c.1950

The Chambers Dictionary, New Edition, Chambers Harrap, 1993

Complete Crossword Companion, Chancellor Press, 1988
      ed. Stibbs, Anne

The Complete Crossword Companion, Chancellor Press, 1988

Crossword Lists and Solver, Bloomsbury Publishing Ltd, 1990

An Exaltation of Larks or The Venereal Game, James Lipton,
      Angus & Robertson Ltd, 1970

A Gaggle of Geese, Philippa-Alys Browne, Barefoot Books, 1995

The Language of Sport, C.E. Hare, Country Life, 1939

A New Dictionary of Birds, Landsborough A. Thompson, (ed.),
      Nelson, 1964

The New First Aid in English, MacIver, Angus, Robert Gibson, c.1970

Usage and Abusage, Eric Partridge, 1947, New and Revised Edition,
      Hamish Hamilton, 1965

The Oxford Reference Dictionary, Clarendon Press, 1986

Dictionary of Phrase and Fable, Nigel Rees, Cassell, 1994

Also published by Merlin Unwin Books

www.merlinunwin.co.uk

Living off the Land Frances Mountford

Make your own Aphrodisiacs Julie and Matthew Bruton Seal

Hedgerow Medicine Julie and Matthew Bruton Seal

Kitchen Medicine Julie and Matthew Bruton Seal

Nature's Playthings Alison Wilson Smith

The Countryside Cartoon Joke Book Roger Penwill

Mushrooming with Confidence Alexander Schwab

The Countryman's Bedside Book BB

Maynard – the Adventures of a Bacon Curer Maynard Davies

The Way of a Countryman Ian Niall